# LIBRARIAN

**Rebecca Hunter**

**Photography by
Chris Fairclough**

**CHERRYTREE BOOKS**

A Cherrytree book

First published in 2005 by
Evans Brothers Ltd
2A Portman Mansions
Chiltern Street
London W1U 6NR

British Library Cataloguing in Publication Data
Hunter, Rebecca
  Librarian. – (People who help us)
  1. Librarians – Juvenile literature
  I. Title
  020

ISBN 1842343017

Planned and produced by Discovery Books Ltd
Editor: Rebecca Hunter
Designer: Ian Winton

**Acknowledgements**
Commissioned photography by Chris Fairclough.

The author, packager and publisher would like to thank the following people for their participation in the book: Staff and clients of the South Eastern Education and Library Service. Staff and pupils of St Mark's Primary School, Belfast, Northern Ireland.

Words appearing in bold **like this**, are explained in the glossary.

# Contents

# I am a librarian

My name is Valerie.
I am a **librarian**.

I work in a library in Belfast,
Northern Ireland.

A library is a place
where books are kept.

Our library is a public library. People can come in and look at the books.

If they find a book they like, they can borrow it and take it home.

A librarian looks after the books and helps people to use the library well.

# Inside the library

**9.00** I arrive at the library.

Many other librarians work here too.
This is Danny. He has been sorting out
the **novels** in the **fiction** section.

A library does not just have books.
It has many other things too.
People come in to read the
newspapers and magazines.

There are also tapes, CDs
and videos to borrow.

There are many computers.
Some are used by adults and
some are especially for children.

# Books on the shelves

This is the children's section of the library. These boys are looking at **information** books.

All information books have a number on their **spine**. The books are put on shelves in **numerical order**.

You can look up a subject on the computer and it will tell you which numbered books to look for.

PEOPLE AT WORK   AT A VET'S    DEBORAH FOX

J
636
089

— number

Story books are stored in a different way. They are put on the shelves in **alphabetical order** using the **author**'s surname.

When a box of new books comes in, I have to sort them out and put them on the right shelves.

# A class comes to the library

Today a class from St Mark's School is visiting the library. I talk to them and tell them what **resources** the library can offer them. Then I give them a **worksheet** to fill in.

They have to look up some of the answers in **reference books**.

Then they write down the answers.

At the end of the visit their teacher reads them a book.

# Selecting new books

About once a month Janet, Michael and I sit round a table and look at the new books that are available. We have to read each one and discuss if we would like to have it in our library.

**12.30** Now it is lunchtime. I always go home for lunch so that I can see my dog Macduff. When it is sunny I eat my lunch in the garden so that Macduff can run around and get some exercise.

# The mobile library

Sometimes I go to visit our **mobile** library. I meet it in town and take some new books. The mobile library is run by Michael and driven by Steve.

The mobile library goes to several villages and is used by over 600 people.

The mobile library is very modern and **well equipped**. It has shelves of books and videos for both adults and children. It also has a computer and **scanner** just like a normal library.

# The Reading Gang

The nearby Laurelhill Library holds a Reading Gang meeting every week. The Reading Gang is for children who really love reading books. We sit in a circle and talk about a book we have all just read.

I give out some question sheets, which ask the children about the book. What did they enjoy most? What didn't they like so much?

At the end of the meeting I show them the book we are going to read next.

# Finding information

Sam and Eamon are doing a school project on Australia. They have come in to the library to find some information about the country. I tell them to ask John to help them.

First John shows them some information about Australia on the computer.

Then John tells them which numbered books to look for. The **contents** page at the front of a book tells them what information is in the book. They can also look up words in the **index**. They write down some useful facts.

# Checking books in and out

Eamon wants to take some books home.
He gives me his **library card**.

I open each book
and scan its **bar
code** with the
computer scanner.
This tells the
computer that the
book is going
out on **loan**.

Then I stamp a date
on the label. This tells
the **borrower** when
to bring the
book back.

This lady has been on holiday so her books are a few days late. She has to pay a **fine**, but it is only 25p!

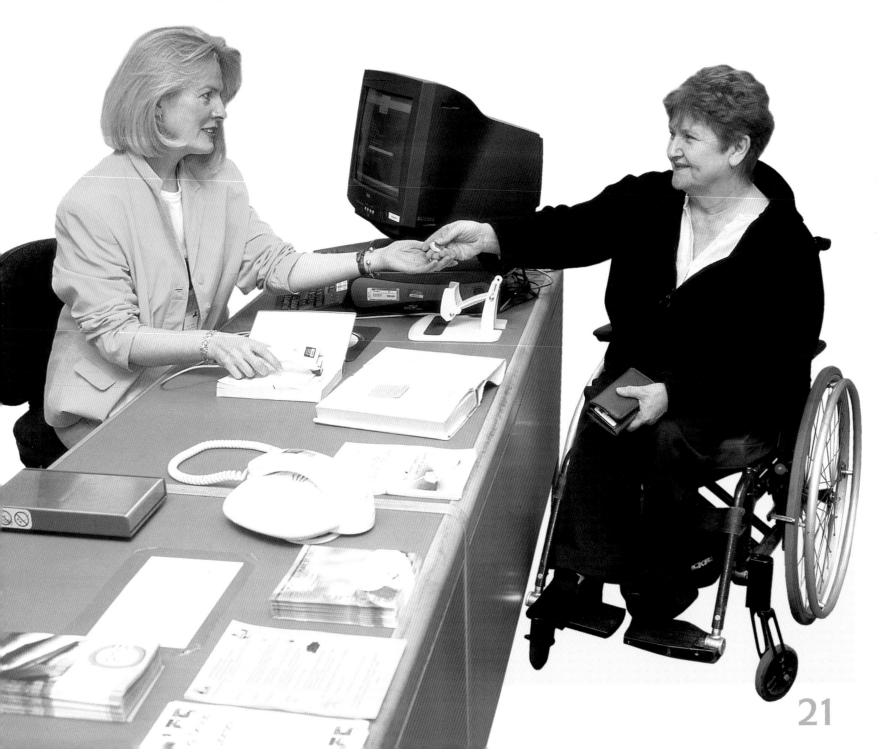

# Going home

**5.00** The library closes. When I have finished my work I can go home.

I enjoy being a librarian. I like helping people find out the information they want. I can only do this because I have a great team of people helping me.

# Glossary

**alphabetical order** sorted by the letters of the alphabet

**author** the person who has written a book

**bar code** a pattern of lines and numbers that can be read by a computer

**borrower** somebody who has been allowed to use something

**contents** a list of things that are in a book

**fiction** stories that are made up

**fine** an amount of money that is paid as a penalty

**index** an alphabetical list of words at the end of a book, with page numbers of where they can be found

**information** facts that are provided or learnt by studying

**librarian** a person who works in a library

**library card** a card that belongs to each member of a library

**loan** something that is being borrowed

**mobile** able to move or be moved easily

**novel** a book that tells a story

**numerical order** sorted by number

**reference book** information book

**resources** useful things that are available to somebody

**scanner** a machine that is used to examine something by moving a beam of light over it

**spine** the edge that faces outwards when a book is on a shelf

**well equipped** full of useful things

**worksheet** a piece of paper with questions to answer

# Index